Pag
Poetry and Blossoms

By

Barbara Carvallo

This is an original work of poetry and photography. All poems and photos are owned exclusively by the author. All photos are of flowers living in my many gardens.

Copyright © 2014 by Barbara Carvallo

Cover Created by Jeff Campanozzi

This book is dedicated to my husband, Bradley, whose unwavering love and compassion make all things possible.

Beltane

The last snow glistens as tender Tulips and Lilies bend under its weight;
softer days are coming; warmer and kinder winds will blow soon.
The world is new now and we the viola and daffodil are waiting
for the time when we will sing our fragrance on the gentle breeze.

May's tender sun glistens on the pristine mantle of snow, warming and melting it deep into the ground to nurture little ones.
The world is new now and we the viola and daffodil are waiting
for the time when we will sing our fragrance on the gentle breeze.

On the cusp of summer, the sweetened air grows warmer by the hour;

Tulips and Lilies stretch their lovely arms and look to the sky.
The world is new now and we the viola and daffodil are waiting
for the time when we will sing our fragrance on the gentle breeze.

Beltane the holiday of union and harmony is upon us;
Sun marries Earth and new life springs forth in myriad shapes and hues.
The world is newly born now and we the viola and daffodil open in the light
for the time is now and we will sing our fragrance on the gentle breeze.

Carnival

In the growing darkness under a clouded Moon, Hecate waits,
Her hounds and raven at Her side listening to the wind.
The howling of the wolves tells of the wild ones gathering;
Shadows of the great cats moving down the ragged summits
with grace and stealth on silent paws proclaim the time is near.

High above the owl, hawk and eagle drift bravely before the veiled Moon,
Muted platinum light frosts the leaves of trees shedding a supernatural glow.
The rabbits and other tiny night creatures nestle in the fallen leaves;
Little ones have no fear of the great predators all around them

for Hecate is near and it is the long-awaited time of Carnival.

As the Moon suddenly sails glittering through the clouds to mark the occasion,
The Great Crone steps out of the night and into the meadow.
In the moonlight growing ever brighter She begins to speak;
"My dear ones I call you together every season on this special night
for most beloved you are in your loyalty and devotion to Me."

At the edge of the circle traced with stardust come the unwanted ones,
Abused, neglected and forgotten they are frightened; it is all they know.
"Come my beloved ones, step into the light with Me;
I am here to heal your wounds, sooth your souls and mend your hearts,
Dance now with your wild cousins and Me; it is Carnival and a day of reckoning is at hand."

I Remember You

I remember you in the sweet air of the early morning,
Lying under the pear tree watching the fat squirrels jump from limb to limb,
With the lazy supremacy of a gracious and unquestioned monarch.

I remember you in the bright white heat of the afternoon,
Stretched out and rolling in the loosened earth beside the pepper plants,
Where the sun struck your slate gray flanks long silver waves ran from head to tail.

I remember you in the cool of the evening,
Walking behind me down the rose garden path,
Relishing the soft advance of night, feline gold eyes shining like the sunset.

I never remember you the way I lost you,
Hideously ill, unresponsive, languid, bewildered,
The power of your slender, supple legs lost to tremors and pain.

I only remember you the way I knew you,
Your courageous heart, gentle spirit, sweet nature,
My ever-constant comrade and serene soul mate.

There is a profound emptiness in the early morning, afternoon and evening,
Under the pear tree, beside the pepper plants, along the rose garden path,
Emptiness mirrored in the heart of your human, your sad and lonely friend.

Imbolc

At the Quickening sister flower and brother tree end their winter sleep,
Brigit calls them to awaken and revel in the lustrous dawn,
Before long they will put on their new green and dance in the balmy wind,
Rich milk will flow from the teats of tender four-legged mothers,
As a new generation suckles close, drinking deep of the liquid of life.

Tall and stately Aspen and Maple prepare to leaf,
Cottonwood and Elm raise their budding arms against a cerulean sky,
For so long I have yearned to hear them whisper words of power,
Hear then sing their gratitude to the rain,
Feel their silhouette gently touch my shoulder as I tend my spring herbs.

Soon I will sleep again in their emerald shade,
And sit without thought of time beneath their elegant canopy,
I will see the sun splatter between their new leaves,
Making stained glass patterns on the greening earth,
Sculpting visions of light and shadow to inspire my daydreams.

In a little while animal and plant will take their place on Brigit's Earth altar,
Under the glowing stars the flawless ritual of blessing will begin,
The Goddess Priestess will draw down the moon,
Shimmering white the flower that shares its name will reflect the alabaster glow,
And another season will begin.

Impressions of Autumn

In Autumn when Goddess wears leaves of gold, rust and crimson in Her hair,
I think most particularly of home, hot soup, cider and fresh bread.
This is the nesting urge that the Great Mother has imprinted on our hearts,
This is the longing to have our loved ones close at hand and safe within our care.

September the sweet month with lingering summer days and deliciously cool evenings,
October the Holy month with the dark night of Samhain approaching in mystery,
November the transitional month with another change of season coming our way,
These are the trappings of Autumn, of Mother Hecate's joyous feast before winter's sleep.

I love Autumn, the early Cronehood of the year, her perfume wood mulch and burnt leaves,
Her cloak a tapestry of mums, orange and black pansies and the last roses of the season.
Secretly she is initiated into the ancient occult wisdom by Mother Hecate,
As she grows white-headed under winter's mantel before our eyes.

In the Moonlight

The Peony glowed,
And Firewitch flared,
Blue Queen Salvia danced,
Red and Yellow Blanket Flower stared.

At the moon, round and full,
Pregnant with ancient knowledge,
In the pale amethyst night,
The Queen of the Witches drifts by.

Fragrant with rose and lavender,
Unseen by the uninitiated eye.

Lydia & Leonard

Lovely little ladybug Lydia,
Sits on a broad leaf of a day,
Awaiting her tender lover Leonard,
To join her in an afternoon of play.

He lands on the leaf behind her,
Touching her antenna with his,
She turns her head and smiles sweetly,
You are beautiful today Lydia he says.

Fly with me to the top of the Maple tree,
Where in a tiny grotto a home I have made,
A place for us to look out on this great world,
Safe and secure in our own private glade.

Away they do fly as fast as they can,
Red speckled wings shimmering in the light,
To their little abode furnished in flowers and leaves,
With piles and pillows of alyssum so white.

Below them an ocean of rose sails by,
A cacophony of color and scent,
Sprayed by a hose fanning high in the air,
Over which a brilliant rainbow is bent.

At the opening of the grotto Goddess' eye appears,
Winking and smiling She holds out Her hand,
Together they fluttered over and sit on Her palm,
Without warning they are much closer to land.

With a nod of Her head they see the rainbow rise,
Tall and wide as a bridge it does grow,
Tenderly She places them in the center of the bridge,
Saying Lydia I am joining you and your beau.

This angry cruel world needs ladybugs,
Of this I am Divinely sure,
Large gentle hearts of gold in tiny frames,
Sacred dwellings of souls so pure.

Make a home and have many little ones,
Cover my Blue Planet with your seed,
I decree you teach the race of humans,
There is much more to life than greed.

Nature's Child

Give me the strength of the mountains and the endurance of the trees,
Let me hear the many wondrous flowers whispering prayers for me.
Allow me to stand in the bright yellow sunlight with the wind in my face,
Let me feel my immortality in the eternity of time and space.
Let me celebrate my humanity in the surf and the moon's silver light,
Give me the knowledge of earth, air, fire, water, day and night.
Allow me to sit beside my loved ones in mellow midnight's hour,
Give me the time to hold them closely as dawn swells with power.

Allow me this closeness to Earth and I will know She and I are one,
Let me draw close to Nature and hear Her say, "Walk with me in the Sun."

On the Divide

In the lusty evening the lilac light is splintered like stained glass,
Filling the spaces between pale saffron peonies and blood-tinged roses.
The wind whispers sweetly to the coming full moon,
Shinning kindly on the indigo blue fissures and ragged peaks of the Great Divide.

This is the breast of the Goddess soon to be sleeping in moonlight,
Breathing in starlight, loving all Her creation with the beauty of Her presence.
Now as mountain streams roll on softly, Hecate steps toward the horizon in ebony and silver,
Obscuring the Divide under a perfect mantel of night.

Unseen the Goddess remains in the song of nocturnal insects,
The sweet scent of the flowers borne on a wandering breeze.
On the currents of piney coolness rolling down off the

Divide,
Her voice fills the growing stillness, "I am with you morning, noon and night."

Ostara

Red-breasted robin perched on the garden gate,
Messenger of Spring singing hello to the daffodils.
Tulips, Siberian Iris and violas are listening as well,
All celebrating the Equinox and the balance of night and day.

The Day of the Trees sees young leaves smudged against an azure sky,
Grass surrounds flower beds in carpets of tender green.
Sunshine falls like lemon drops on the new crimson leaves of the rose,
Nature is reborn in the elegance of Spring.

Lush Summer will follow Spring dressed in roses and herbs,

Eostre the Maiden will become the Great Mother of all life.
Days will lengthen out in long, lazy avenues of light,
Darkness will flow through a river of moon glow and earthy scents.

In the sparkling newness of Spring the world is the Goddess' only child,
Crocus, astilbe and lilacs are the magical toys in the nursery.
Bleeding Heart and Lily of the Valley hang like magic mobiles before the honeybees' eyes,
All is good, all is well and the remarkable beauty of the Earth is untarnished.

Owl

In the mystery and wonder of Goddess' night
Owl spreads her great wings and takes to flight.
Full moon lavishes silver on Owl's path at night
As she dives and glides in her spectacular flight.

Darkness the glory of Goddess' night
For Owl is the medium of perfect sight.
Eyes lit with wisdom in silvery night
Awareness unimaginable to human sight.

Hecate the Goddess who rules sacred night
Embraces with darkness Owl's elegant flight.
As moonlit wings caress the soul of night
Goddess and Owl are one in flight.

Samhain

Now is the time of the last and best harvest of the year
The time the Crone and Sage reverently call Samhain,
When the veil between the worlds is thin and Hecate is near
Ancient rites are celebrated and great magic is seen.

In the buttery sunlight of the late afternoon
Rusty golden leaves drift silently to the ground.
Smoky beginnings of bonfires that will flame soon
Linger under the breath of hot cider drifting around.

Sunset runs like liquid amber over the mighty Collegiate Range
Soon the Rockies will sleep heavily under a frosty lace cloak.
Winter's loving embrace brings silence, deep slumber and change
Meditation, introspection and contemplation for Pagan folk.

Samhain to Samhain the Wheel turns without beginning or end
Day and night chasing one another around our Planet Divine.
Season to season the Earth renews its life force time and again,
As Hecate walks the Circle shifting the seasons with delicate signs.

At moonrise the children run costumed questing for sweets
The faithful gather around their altars in coven and alone.
Candlelight and starlight marry along energy charged streets,
For all on this New Year's night the whole universe is home.

Mother Hecate enters the hearts of Her children opening their eyes
The veil is thinning as the Ancients and precious lost ones draw near.
One more chance to say I love you and until next Samhain goodbye,
It is bittersweet to touch memories and tearfully watch them disappear.

Hecate walks among her children as velvet midnight tenderly advances
Touching each and planting a seed of enlightenment for harvesting next year.
Nourished by faith in Goddess, mind and spirit garden in dreams and dances,
Watered by the wisdom of the Old Ones tiny seeds grow toward a brighter frontier.

Sounds of Summer

Silver chimes ring softly in the supple and pleasant breeze,
Small blue irises and yellow daffodils open their eyes to see,
The lemon colored sunshine rolling down the Great Divide,
As into the garden the gentle Fae come running side by side.

"This is the beginning of the season," they sing in elegant harmony,
"It is time to till soil, prune roses and plant seeds one, two, three,"
The most magically skilled gardeners on the face of Goddess' Earth,
With lutes, cymbals and voices so rare helping the garden give birth.

Soon the delphinium rises tall, listening to bluebirds in the dazzling pear tree,
Silken pansies nestled near the ground hear the ladybugs flying free,
Wildflowers dancing in gorgeous chaos, love the sound of rain best of all,
But Her Majesty the Rose opens her fabulous blooms only at Goddess' call.

The Color of the Rain

I saw the rain fall to the ground,
Touched softly gold by a hidden sun,
Settle on the magenta face of an open rose,
Like grateful teardrops.

I saw the crimson tinted rain fall,
Between the autumn leaves of the delicate Aspen,
Caressing the Rocky Mountains,
With the Goddess' Divine passion.

I saw the rain fall crystalline white,
On a frozen landscape,
Where all life slept peacefully,
In suspended animation under a blue-gray sky.

I saw the rain fall tender green,
Kissing blossoms and slender shoots,
Wrapped in the Goddess' life-giving embrace,
And the Earth was clean and bright and new once again.

The Flight of the Crone

In the cool, still, velvety night,
By the dark of the moon in silver starlight,
The Crone raises Her cloak and takes to flight.

High above the slumbering, shadowy ground,
She sores through the trees without a sound,
For company a raven and a three-headed hound.

In a voice deep as darkness She begins to sing,
Ancient words of power with solemnity ring,
I am the Goddess; I am Magic on the Wing.

The Old Weathered Fence

Elegant shrub stands tall and sun soaked
Exhaling rose into the early summer breeze,
Behind her stands a fence of weathered wood
Grateful for the chance to feel her breathe.

To hear her stir the silver chimes with her sweet scent
Rippling the clear, cool water in the old stone birdbath,
Where tiny crimson climbers cling lovingly to the lip
Before gracefully draping down to line the garden path.

Near her and clustering large in their red clay pots
Velvety pansies with faces of sapphire and gold,
Are the first to notice clouds gathering overhead
Sensing the breeze flee before the wind so bold.

The blossom laden shrub slips quickly into shade
Holding her rosy breath and awaiting the storm,
Behind her the old fence shutters and sways,
As the mighty West Wind blows wet and warm.

Silver chimes sound a single perfect note
The melodic rain blissfully begins to fall,
Gathering power like a Puccini aria
Lending a grand passion to a simple summer squall.

Suddenly wind goes silent, rain stops and clouds clear
The brilliant yellow-white sun embraces the Earth,
Touching each leaf and flower with tenderness and joy
Exhilaration, delight, health and welcome rebirth.

Elegant shrub stands tall and rain soaked
Exhaling a breath of rose into the sparkling afternoon,
Behind her stands a fence of weathered wood,
Feeling young and hopeful, praying the rain returns soon.

The Old Ones Speak

When I see the Blessed Moon gowned in silvery light
Drifting through the ebony sky cloudy with star dust,
I see the hills of Ireland drenched in the fog of time,
I see my grandmothers worshiping that ancient land
Healing, comforting, advising their ancient people;
Even as they midwife and support those who must crossover
They honor the Goddess Cerridwen,
They tend Her cauldron of life and death.

I see the men in long black gowns coming for them
Swelling out of the shadows on a wave of self righteousness,
In service to an angry god they come with Bible and fire,
To torture, burn and drowned Cerridwen's daughters
Saying that to accept their angry god is salvation;
But not from the cruelty, lies and murder hidden in their

vestments
They rob for profit those they kill as they preach forgiveness,
For when was such a Church ever built without commerce?

Through shadowy trees my ancestors whisper in the Sacred Night
To a daughter who need not fear the Bible or the torch,
Be careful as you go in a world of angry gods say they,
In words deepened by centuries of generational harmony
They sigh, honor the Goddess and know the Craft;
To be free you must think free and never doubt the path
Some will trivialize your knowledge and demonize your faith,
It is their own darkness they fear and only they can light their way.

The Purple Tulip

Bright glowing purple the royal color,
Of the pointed tulip shaped like a crown,
Sitting beside the old rose trellis,
Closing slowly as the sun goes down.

In twilight purple turns ebony,
As the tulip folds gently into the night,
Other flowers of myriad colors,
Wait to be kissed again by the light.

Morning finds the tulip missing,
Lifted from her stem without a trace,
Rose trellis saw the abduction,
Saw the tulip lifted from her place.

Tell us trellis the flowers whisper,
Who took the lovely tulip from her stem,
It was the Fae the ancient trellis answers,
Dozens, no hundreds of them.

They came and took the purple tulip,
Then flew away without a sound,
Their queen wants this lovely flower,
To wear forever and ever as her crown.

The White Wolf

In moonlight White Wolf steps over sparkling snow,
The sterling night glistens with a winter white glow,
From the shadows she strolls into shimmering light,
Through a Pine and Spruce lined clearing ever so bright.

All around her peaks of granite rise toward the sky,
Dressed in ebony fissures crowned with flickering eyes,
From between the Spruce a great figure lands on the Earth,
Goddess Hecate has come to help the White Wolf give birth.

"Beautiful wolf why are you alone, your time is near,
Soon the birthing will begin your mate must be here."
"Mother, he readies a warm den for the young ones to sleep,
Safe from Winter's frozen mantel so pale and so deep."

Sacred darkness fractures at the base of a tall Pine,
Midnight coat and green eyes under the blessed moon

shine,
Standing tall and looking majestically from left to right,
He moves forward bringing with him the power of the night.

He bows his head solemnly to the Goddess attending his mate,
Nuzzles White Wolf's neck tenderly and prepares to wait,
The first pain is staggering and brings her to the ground,
Hecate waves Her arm above the snow, it softens like down.

Crone Goddess places Her hand on White Wolf's brow,
"I am with you little one and the time is now."
In the moonlight brilliant crimson pools on pristine white snow,
Four little cubs enter the world very soft and all aglow.

"Gather these little ones, take them back to your den,
Begin the process of rearing and teaching cubs again,
Teach them to protect and hunt and sense extremely well,
To the murderers these magic creatures bring a special kind of hell."

"White Wolf and her mate shall remain in this country beyond time,
Tall jagged peaks, shimmering moonlight, pale snow, and sweet Pine,
They are my children, my beloved and my kin,
The world of man shall never see them again."

Yule

Far above the city in a canyon of stone,
Among Pine, Fur and Spruce I stand alone.
Snow covered peaks soar high above,
Moonlight covers all with Goddess' love.

In a sacred place I clear snow from stone,
Preparing my Yule log to welcome the Crone.
Red and gold fire radiates Goddess' love,
Snapping and dancing, sending sparks high above.

In starlight wings cast shadow on stone,
I realize suddenly that I am not alone.
As the fire grows brighter, I see high above,
Snowy Owl bringing wisdom and Goddess' love.

Graceful as Aspen a Deer emerges from stone,
Silver Antlers glittering he stands proud and alone.

Stag of myth and Lord of legend brings Goddess' love,
Stepping forward slowly he glances high above.

Mountain Cat drifts forward casting shadow on stone,
In power and majesty she stands silent and alone.
Living with perfect dignity in the mountains high above,
Her beautiful sovereignty a symbol of Goddess' love.

Sadly, I whisper to the noble ones in the canyon of stone,
Dear friends, I have no gifts to offer you I am poor and alone.
The only thing I can share with you is Goddess' love,
And in peace and gratitude, the Earth below and Moon above.

Unfathomable as eternity a voice ricochets off stone,
You are my daughter; you are never poor or alone.
The wild ones came to be with you and share My love,
To join you in ritual and worship under the stars above.

The Goddess commands the stars toward the canyon of stone,
Down they fall onto the tree branches in clusters and alone.
It is Yule my children and you shall feast in My love,
You shall find your gifts by the light of the moon above.

Made in the USA
Columbia, SC
28 May 2023